APE ESCAPES!

And More True Stories of Animals Behaving Badly

Published by the National Geographic Society

John M. Fahey, Jr., *Chairman of the Board and Chief Executive Officer*

Timothy T. Kelly, *President*

Declan Moore, *Executive Vice President; President, Publishing and Digital Media*

Melina Gerosa Bellows, *Executive Vice President; Chief Creative Officer, Books, Kids, and Family*

Prepared by the Book Division

Hector Sierra, *Senior Vice President and General Manager*

Nancy Laties Feresten, *Senior Vice President, Editor in Chief, Children's Books*

Jonathan Halling, *Design Director, Books and Children's Publishing*

Jay Sumner, *Director of Photography, Children's Publishing*

Jennifer Emmett, *Editorial Director, Children's Books*

Eva Absher-Schantz, *Managing Art Director, Children's Books*

Carl Mehler, *Director of Maps*

R. Gary Colbert, *Production Director*

Jennifer A. Thornton, *Director of Managing Editorial*

Staff for This Book

Becky Baines, *Project Editor*

Lisa Jewell, *Illustrations Editor*

Eva Absher, *Art Director*

Ruthie Thompson, *Designer*

Grace Hill, *Associate Managing Editor*

Joan Gossett, *Production Editor*

Lewis R. Bassford, *Production Manager*

Susan Borke, *Legal and Business Affairs*

Kate Olesin, *Assistant Editor*

Kathryn Robbins, *Design Production Assistant*

Hillary Moloney, *Illustrations Assistant*

Manufacturing and Quality Management

Christopher A. Liedel, *Chief Financial Officer*

Phillip L. Schlosser, *Senior Vice President*

Chris Brown, *Vice President*

George Bounelis, *Vice President, Production Services*

Nicole Elliott, *Manager*

Rachel Faulise, *Manager*

Robert L. Barr, *Manager*

The National Geographic Society is one of the world's largest nonprofit scientific and educational organizations. Founded in 1888 to "increase and diffuse geographic knowledge," the Society works to inspire people to care about the planet. National Geographic reflects the world through its magazines, television programs, films, music and radio, books, DVDs, maps, exhibitions, live events, school publishing programs, interactive media and merchandise. *National Geographic* magazine, the Society's official journal, published in English and 33 local-language editions, is read by more than 38 million people each month. The National Geographic Channel reaches 320 million households in 34 languages in 166 countries. National Geographic Digital Media receives more than 15 million visitors a month. National Geographic has funded more than 9,400 scientific research, conservation, and exploration projects and supports an education program promoting geography literacy. For more information, visit nationalgeographic.com.

For more information, please call
1-800-NGS LINE (647-5463) or
write to the following address:
National Geographic Society
1145 17th Street N.W.
Washington, D.C. 20036-4688 U.S.A.

Visit us online at nationalgeographic.com/books

For librarians and teachers: ngchildrensbooks.org

More for kids from National Geographic:
kids.nationalgeographic.com

For information about special discounts for bulk purchases, please contact National Geographic Books Special Sales:
ngspecsales@ngs.org

For rights or permissions inquiries, please contact National Geographic Books Subsidiary Rights: ngbookrights@ngs.org

Trade paperback ISBN: 978-1-4263-0936-6
Reinforced library edition ISBN:
978-1-4263-0955-7

Printed in China
12/RRDS/1

Table of CONTENTS

Fu as a 250-pound (114 kg) "pasha." A pasha is a full-grown male with cheek pads.

FU MANCHU: APE ESCAPES!

In the wild, baby orangutans like this one stay with their moms eight years or more.

A SCAMP IS BORN

July 1965, Omaha, Nebraska

A young orangutan peers out of his cage at the Henry Doorly Zoo. No humans are in sight. The coast is clear.

He sticks his long fingers through the chain-link fence. He bends back one corner. He pulls. *ZZIIIIP!* The stiff metal fencing unravels like a hand-knit scarf.

Some time later, veterinarian Lee Simmons arrives at work. He rounds a bend in the path and *yikes!* Dr. Simmons stops in his tracks. It couldn't be, but it is. A shaggy, red-haired ape sits up in a tree. *How did he get loose?*

The ape is about six years old, tailless, and weighs 100 pounds (45 kg). He has a mustache and beard like a famous movie character. For that reason he is called Fu Manchu. Fu's arms are super strong and longer than most fourth graders are tall. In a wrestling match against a man, the orangutan would win.

The ape doesn't move or make a sound. But Dr. Simmons sees a twinkle in his eyes. The vet can't help but wonder if Fu knew what he was doing. *It's like he's been sitting there just waiting for me.*

Fu climbs down. The sun sparkles on his red hair as he scrambles back to his cage. Dr. Simmons follows, shaking his head. *What a crazy ape!* He locks Fu inside. He calls someone to fix the fence and then goes about his normal business. And Fu goes about his—dreaming up more hijinks to come.

Fu was born in a rain forest on the Indonesian island of Sumatra (sounds like SUE-MAH-TRA). Like most baby orangutans, Fu probably never knew his father. Orangutan mothers care for their helpless babies. Fu's mother nursed him. She held him and snuggled him. Every night she built them a nest high in the treetops.

These sleeping nests were the size of

Did You Know?

For the first few weeks after they're born, baby orangutans cling to their moms' bellies.

bathtubs. Fu's mother made them by twisting leafy branches together. Each fresh, new nest must have felt as comfy to Fu as clean bedsheets do to you.

Usually Fu and his mom stayed dry in their cozy bed in the sky. At other times thunder boomed. Rain fell in sheets. Then the apes huddled together and turned giant leaves into umbrellas.

During the day, Fu often rode on his mother's back. He clutched her hair as they swung through the trees looking for durian (sounds like DUR-EE-ANN) fruits. Durian fruits stink like sweaty gym socks. But orangutans go ape for the smelly stuff.

The problem is durian fruits don't all

ripen at the same time, and the trees are scattered. To find them, orangutans must keep a map of the forest inside their heads. For Fu's mother it must have been like memorizing a school bus route with hundreds of stops.

Finding water was easier. It collects in hollow tree trunks after a rain. Fu might have gotten a drink by scooping water out with a folded leaf. Or maybe he chewed leaves into a sort of sponge. Then he sopped up water and dripped it into his mouth. Either way, Fu used leaves as tools.

Long ago, Indonesian people dubbed these clever apes "orangutans." In their language the word *orang* means

Did You Know?

As baby orangutans get older, they ride "piggyback" to get a better view of their surroundings.

"person" and *utan* means "forest."
Together you get "person of the forest."

One day Fu and his mother heard strange sounds in the swamp. Hunters had entered the jungle. They carried axes and homemade nets on their backs. Rivers of sweat ran down the men's bare chests. Armies of insects buzzed in their faces. But nothing stopped them. The men were animal collectors. They feed their families by catching and selling wild animals. A baby orangutan will get them a lot of money.

Did Fu's mother know they wanted her baby? Probably not, but she sensed danger. She swung from limb to limb, snapping off branches. She threw the branches down on the hunters.

Orangutans and Tools

Orangutans are the smartest of all the great apes. They learn new things quickly. Because of this, people have spent years studying orangutans and learning more about them. Orangutans have been seen in the wild and in zoos using tools to scratch themselves; cover themselves from the rain; collect water, honey, or bugs for food; swat stinging insects; and spear fish in the water.

The animal collectors looked up. The mother ape looked like a tiny black doll hanging against the blue sky. Was she holding a baby?

The hunters had a traditional way of catching orangutans. They didn't try to climb up after them. Not at first. That might have spooked the ape into escaping through the treetops. Instead, the animal collectors formed a circle. They pulled out their axes and hacked away at tree trunks.

The ground shook as a tall tree crashed to the forest floor. Then a second one, and a third. The trees were so close together that each one that fell knocked down another. CHOP! CHOP! The men worked their way to the last tree—the one holding the apes.

"*Pzz squee.*" Fu's mother squeaked and ran, looking for a way to escape. Seeing none, she moved far out on a limb.

A man climbed way, way up the smooth trunk. He broke off a leafy branch and shook it at her.

Fu's mother probably did what most orangutans do when cornered by hunters. She smacked her lips. Her black eyes shone with fear. With one man in the tree and more below, she first scrambled up and then down. Up and then down.

Suddenly the scared ape leaped to the ground. With her baby hugging her belly, she ran for her life. But the men ran faster.

The boss hunter yelled. He ordered his men to throw their nets.

SWOOSH! The apes were trapped!

Fu, always the practical joker, loved performing for happy, smiling zoo visitors.

Chapter 2

HERO Prankster

The animal collectors have gotten what they came for. They carry Fu out of the jungle and ship him to Singapore. They put him up for sale in the marketplace. Except for his fur, the little red ape looks much like a human baby. An American man has come to buy animals for a zoo in Louisiana. He likes the look of Fu. The American has already spent a lot of money on rare parrots, monkeys, pythons, and crocodiles. Now he buys Fu.

Fu spends three years in Louisiana. Then he is sent to Omaha, Nebraska.

In the wild, Fu swung from branches and hung from vines. Thumbs on his feet as well as his hands helped him hang on. Sometimes he went two weeks without touching the ground.

Life is different in a zoo. Soon after Fu arrives in Omaha, the zookeepers build a large, modern Great Ape House. But only a few trees grow in the Ape House yard. They are nothing like the giant trees that grow packed together in the rain forest. Fu can't build a sleeping nest in them. There is no tangled jungle for him to learn his way around. But the most important difference is food. Here a zookeeper brings him supper in a bowl. Fu does not need to find his own meals. He does not need to memorize 1,000 different kinds of plants like his mom did.

Like a bored kid in school, Fu turns his mind to other things. When a tree dies in his yard, Fu pulls it apart. He gathers up two chunks of wood and sets them against the building. They make a ramp that he can climb.

"There's an ape on the roof!" shouts a zoo visitor.

Dr. Simmons rushes to the scene. "Fu," he orders, hands on his hips. "Come down from there."

Fu ignores him. The naughty ape scrambles across the roof and wraps

his hairy arms around the chimney.
CAARACK! He tears it off the roof and
flings it over the edge!

That does it. Zookeeper Jerry Stones
has had enough. Maybe he can help the
bored ape stay out of
trouble. He will give Fu
something to swing on.

Jerry goes inside the
orangutan's cage and
hangs a chain from one
wall to another. Fu sits quietly in a corner
and pretends not to notice, but the tricky
ape is secretly watching the whole time.

Looks good, Jerry thinks, when he
finishes. He packs up his tools and leaves,
banging the door behind him.

The next morning Jerry returns to

admire his work. But when he enters the ape house, he just stands there in shock! The steel chain he had so carefully hung lies in a pile on the floor. Fu stands beside it—holding the screws in his fist.

Grumbling, Jerry rehangs the chain. Then he pulls out his hammer. WHAM! He flattens the end of each screw.

Not even Fu can take them out now, he thinks.

A month goes by. Jerry forgets the mischief. He goes to the Ape House to give Fu some monkey biscuits and . . . gasp! The heavy chain lies on the floor like a broken necklace. *How on earth?*

Fu was sneaky. He must have spent weeks turning those screws when no one was looking.

"Doggone it, Fueey," mutters Jerry. He grabs a ladder and tools.

CLATTER! CLANK! BANG! Jerry hangs the chain for the third time.

Fu is naughty all right, but he is also kind. On another day Dr. Simmons and a second man are working together inside Fu's cage. The floor is wet. The other man slips and sticks out his hand to catch himself. He accidentally touches the big picture window that separates Fu from zoo visitors.

ZAP!

An electric shock knocks the man across the room. He lands curled up on the floor.

Fu rushes to help. First, he looks over the shaken man for injuries. Then he straightens out the man's finger. Finally, he leads him to the window.

The window is electrified to keep Fu from smudging the glass. But one little strip is safe to touch, and Fu knows it. The smart ape places the man's finger there. It is like he is saying, "Next time, touch here. Then you won't get hurt."

Fu made zoo officials want more apes like him. But the Indonesian government passed a law protecting orangutans. Catching, killing, and selling them was illegal. That left one solution. They had to find Fu a girl orangutan.

Zookeepers put Fu and another orangutan named "Tondelayo" together. The two apes hit it off right away, but Tondelayo doesn't like Jerry. She paces and her lips tighten whenever he enters their cage. He feels uneasy around her.

One day it happens.

Jerry is feeding Tondelayo when she suddenly sinks her teeth into his leg! She bites through his rubber boot, wool pants, and heavy socks. "Arghh!" Jerry screams. Trying to get away, he whacks Tondelayo in the head with the rubber feed bucket.

She lets go.

With his leg bleeding, Jerry hops to safety.

Fu had done nothing. But weeks later Tondelayo attacks again. This time Fu is ready. He jumps on his mate and bites her hard. Tondelayo squeaks and backs off. She never hurts Jerry again.

If you give an ape an iPad...

They finger-paint, watch home videos, and look at books, says Trish Khan. Trish is a zookeeper at Wisconsin's Milwaukee County Zoo. She says orangutans are so intelligent that they need to be introduced to new things. Otherwise they get bored.

Trish thinks someone should design a kind of Facebook app for apes. Using it, an orangutan could touch another ape's photo and watch a live cam of that ape in action.

"The things that interest kids also interest an orangutan," says Khan. Imagine if you could play Flick Kick Football on your phone with an ape!

Once Fu mastered the art of the escape, it was time to teach the other orangutans how to misbehave.

Chapter 3

Wise Guy Ape

"Jerry! Jerry! The orangutans are out!"

Jerry Stones is now head zookeeper. He hears the shouts, but it takes a minute for the words to sink in. When they do, he jumps up from his desk and races outside.

"Over there! In the trees." A visitor points to a group of elms on a hill near the elephant barn. It is late fall, and their leaves have dropped. Jerry spots what looks like five big, hairy apes sitting on the bare branches.

Not waiting for help, Jerry scrambles up one of the trees as if he were an ape himself. He takes one orangutan by the hand and leads him back to the Ape House. Jerry does this again and again, until he has everybody back where they belong. Now Jerry must figure out how they escaped.

One thing he knows already. Fu was behind it. He let himself out and then snapped off the padlocks on the other apes' cages. But how did he do it? Jerry checks the Ape House yard for anything strange.

After a while, he looks into a deep ditch that works like a fence. In the bottom, at

one end of the ditch, is a door. This door
leads into the basement of the Ape House.
But it is not an ordinary door. This door is
meant to be secure, so it doesn't have an
outside handle. It can only be opened from
the inside by someone using a key.

But it's open! *Aha!* Jerry thinks. *Some
careless keeper forgot to lock it.* He steps
inside. The place is a mess. Dirt covers the
floor, and there are pipes thrown about.
Jerry follows the trail. It leads to a ladder.
The apes had climbed up to the first floor.
Then they simply pushed open the big glass
doors and walked out into the sun.

Jerry warns the keepers. "Do not let
this happen again!"

But happen it does—the very next
week. And again the week after that!

After the third breakout, Jerry says that he will fire the person who left the door open.

That's when he and a keeper spot Fu in the ditch. Three other apes are gathered around watching over his shoulder. Fu slips a little wire under the lock, and like magic, the door swings open.

The men run into the building and block the apes from coming up the ladder. Jerry takes away Fu's "key" and returns everyone to their cages. "From now on," Jerry says, "keepers will sweep the ditch every day. They'll rake the grass and search under bushes for wires."

He thinks the problem is solved.

But weeks later, Jerry spots something shiny poking out of Fu's mouth. "Open up, Fueey," Jerry says. Fu does, and Jerry sticks in his finger. He feels around and pulls out guess what. Another piece of wire! The sneaky ape has bent it like a horseshoe to fit in his mouth!

But there's one question left. Where is Fu getting these wires?

One day Dr. Simmons goes to the Ape House. He finds Fu lying on his side reaching through the bars. *Now what's he up to?* Dr. Simmons stays out of sight and watches.

A female orangutan named Heavy Lamar lives next door to Fu. Dr. Simmons has her on a diet because she is too fat. Pretty soon the vet sees Heavy's hairy arm slide from around the corner. She and Fu touch hands, and Fu slips Heavy a monkey biscuit. In return, Heavy gives him a piece of wire. The wire is from a screen that covers the lightbulb hanging in her cage.

They have their answer.

Jerry and his crew scurry around securing the Ape House. They screw steel plates on the doors to the orangutan cages. That way Fu can't twist off the locks. They smooth out the sides of the ditch so no orangutan can climb it. They fix the light screen in Heavy's cage.

This time their work pays off. The ape escapes stop.

Lovable Fu is a 250-pound (114 kg) "pasha" now. Pashas are full-grown males and have cheek flaps and a big throat pouch. The throat pouch helps Fu make the "long call." This is a sound that can be heard from over a mile (1.6 km) away.

As big as Fu is, Bornean (sounds like BORE-NEE-ANN) orangutans grow even larger. The males have even bigger cheek flaps. In 1983, the Omaha zoo had Bornean and Sumatran orangutans. The people in charge later decided to focus on just one kind—the Bornean apes. Because Fu is from Sumatra, they sent him to the Gladys Porter Zoo in Texas.

In Texas, Fu becomes a big shot all over again—but for another reason. He is the only male in a group of females. Before his death in 1992, Fu fathered twenty babies. So far, none of them has pulled any such silly stunts as their father did. But who knows? One of them still might.

Orangutan Friends

In the wild, orangutans usually live alone. But they occasionally get together in groups, and mom orangutans spend years raising their young (unlike many other animals). Scientists think that this means they live alone because they have to. In the wild, their food is scattered and hard to find. Orangutans in groups would have a harder time getting enough to eat. In zoos, orangutans seem to not mind each other's company. Fu and Heavy were friends and even helped each other.

Some people wonder. *Did Fu's many escapes mean he hated zoo life?* Probably not. The mischief-loving ape ate good meals. He could go inside out of the rain to be warm and dry. He seemed to enjoy playing in his yard, helping raise his babies, and showing off for visitors.

But there is stronger proof. No matter how many times Fu broke out of his cage, he never left the zoo grounds. The clever ape always came back.

Maybe Fu never intended to run away. Maybe he liked using his brain and simply enjoyed playing jokes.

Curtis and Peggy sit together on a hill near their home in the United Kingdom.

PEGGY:
THE MISCHIEVOUS PUP

Peggy loves to jump. Here she jumps for a stick that Curtis tries to hold out of her reach.

Chapter 1

April 2007,
Northumberland, England

Peggy the mutt lifts her black, wet nose in the air. *Sniff! Sniff!* Something smells yummy! She jumps to her feet and runs into the kitchen. The lady of the house has just pulled a baked ham out of the oven.

Peggy flops down in the middle of the tiny room. The busy woman almost trips over her. "Go away,

Peggy!" she orders. "This isn't for you."
But Peggy stays. Every little while, she
inches closer to the prize. A puddle of dog
drool forms on the floor.

Suddenly *BRR-IIING! BRR-IIING!*
The telephone rings. The lady forgets about
Peggy and hurries to answer it.

Big mistake.

The waiting dog grabs the ham as quick
as a frog catching a fly. Two gulps and it's
gone! Every last bit! Full and happy, Peggy
lies down and licks her mouth.

This doesn't please the woman's hungry
family. They have only bread and veggies
for dinner!

Peggy belongs to Tony and Lorraine
Shaw and their sons, Daniel, six, and
Curtis, seven. Mr. Shaw rescued Peggy

from an old junkyard. Now they all live together in a three-bedroom house beside the North Sea. Curtis loves the mutt and plays with her a lot. But even he admits she's naughty—has been ever since his dad brought her home. Take the problem with the laundry, for example.

Mrs. Shaw used to hang her wash on the line. One day Peggy ran, jumped, and tore it down. Wooden clothes-pegs flew through the air as Peggy yanked down shirts, pants, and underwear. *Snap! Snap!* More clothes dropped. More pegs popped. In minutes, all the wash lay on the ground. Why? Peggy loved to chew on the pegs.

"Bad dog," Mrs. Shaw said.

The guilty puppy stopped chewing. She lowered her head and laid back her ears. Her eyelids drooped. She didn't mean to be bad.

But what happened the next time Mrs. Shaw hung out wet clothes? The little rascal yanked them down again. Mrs. Shaw saw the mess and sighed. She put her hands on her hips.

"If you like clothes-pegs this much," she said, "that's what we'll name you—Peggy."

The floppy-eared, black and brown troublemaker is part Rottweiler and part German shepherd. Her paws are big as plates. "She is soft all over like a teddy bear," says Curtis. But the best thing about her? She makes him laugh.

The gleeful sound of Curtis laughing

brightens the entire Shaw household. It especially makes Mr. and Mrs. Shaw happy. Curtis has many health problems. He can't eat snacks made with eggs or nuts because his throat will swell shut. Sometimes he finds it hard to breathe. There is also something different about Curtis's brain that makes his mind wander. He doesn't listen well. He squirms in his seat, and he talks too loud. This makes him a target for bullies.

Before Peggy came, Curtis often acted angry or sad. He didn't have many friends.

Now he has a buddy in Peggy. At home she follows him everywhere. She listens to everything he says and never argues or talks back. As Mr. Shaw explains, "She just loves Curtis to bits." But guess what?

Peggy may be the world's naughtiest dog.

Her stunts can be silly or serious. Peggy jumps up on people. Curtis yells and tries to stop her. But he might as well try to stop a speeding train. Peggy gets so excited when visitors come to the house that she charges into them. She only wants to say hello, but sometimes she knocks people flat. If she gets really excited, she loses control and pees on their feet.

"Sorry," says Curtis.

"Ewww," say the visitors.

Everyone living with Peggy must pick up their things. Besides clothes-pegs, she chews on soccer balls. She sneaks upstairs and eats the stuffing out of teddy bears. She even chews on table legs. From socks to spider plants, the Shaws follow one rule. "Put it up high or say goodbye!"

When Peggy isn't chewing, she's barking. She barks at strangers. She barks at birds. She barks at most anything that moves.

And that's not all she does. Peggy eats so much that she grows faster than Pinocchio's nose. She gobbles the food Curtis pours in her dish. Then she pokes her head into the bag looking for more. She eats frozen peas out of the package and smelly garbage in the trash can. Her worst food prank is still stealing the ham.

After pigging out on the family's supper that night, Peggy snuffles around wanting a cuddle. Curtis doesn't feel like cuddling. He'd rather have ham. The puppy paws at his knee. Curtis looks away. She pushes her head under his hand and cries for attention. "I'm mad at you," Curtis says. The puppy puts her paws on his shoulders. *Slurp.*

Curtis giggles and wipes his chin.

"Oh, all right," he says and pulls her into his lap.

But minutes later . . . "Pee-yew!" Curtis pulls his shirt up over his nose. Eating people food makes Peggy pass gas.

Curtis waves at the air. "Bad dog," he grumbles.

Peggy grins and thumps her tail on the floor.

Mr. and Mrs. Shaw can't help themselves. They love the goofy mutt. So does Daniel. Curtis loves her most of all. But one day Peggy's troublemaking goes too far. You might even say it "takes the cake."

All About Dogs

1. All dogs descend from wolves.
2. A 6.6-pound (3 kg) Chihuahua named Momo is the world's smallest search and rescue dog.
3. A dog's nose print is as individual as a human's fingerprint.
4. Dogs are the most varied species. They come in hundreds of shapes and sizes.
5. Chaser the Border collie may be the world's smartest dog. He knows the names of more than 1,000 objects.
6. A Labrador retriever–poodle mix is called a Labradoodle.
7. "Trouble," a white Maltese, is richer than most people. He inherited $12 million.

Peggy and Mrs. Shaw show off the biggest mess Peggy ever made.

It's Mr. Shaw's 46th birthday. To celebrate, Mrs. Shaw buys a chocolate cake. White icing spells out "Happy Birthday" across the top. The baker packs the cake in a bakery box, and Mrs. Shaw carries it home. The Shaw family must wait to enjoy it later. They are due at school for a meeting with Curtis's teacher.

Mrs. Shaw hunts for a hiding place in her small kitchen. Finally

she tucks the cake on a shelf high above
the stove. *Peggy will never get it up here,*
she figures. Then she hears a buzzer. The
laundry is done. Mrs. Shaw bends down
and pulls a pile of warm towels out of the
dryer. She dumps them on the counter next
to the stove.

"Come on, boys," she says. "Let's go."

Curtis pushes Peggy off his lap. "Be a
good dog," he says. "We won't be gone long."

The whole family heads out the door.
Mr. Shaw leaves last. He turns the bolt and
tugs the door to make sure it's locked.
They will stop at his mother's house on the
way. Nana will watch the kids while he
and Mrs. Shaw go to the meeting.

No sooner does the family leave than
Peggy follows her nose into the kitchen.

Mrs. Shaw hid the cake, but "out of sight, out of mind" does not work for dogs. Peggy sniffs everything, and her brain is one big filing cabinet full of odors. Her sense of smell is so powerful that she knows people, places, and animals by scent—not by their looks. Now Peggy smells cake!

She jumps for it like she jumps for clothes-pegs. One big leap and Peggy knocks the cake down with her snout. She also accidentally moves the pile of towels. Some of them land on a stove burner. Does Peggy also bump the knob and turn the burner on? Or did Mrs. Shaw forget to turn it off in her hurry to leave? It doesn't matter. Minutes pass. Smoke rises from the pile of towels. Then . . .

FIRE!

Red and orange flames shoot toward the ceiling. They crackle and hiss. Thick black smoke chokes the air. It makes it hard for Peggy to breathe. *Woof! Woof! Ayyoooo!* She howls for help.

Peggy's cries alert the man living on the other side of their two-family house. He comes over to see what's wrong and discovers the fire.

The neighbor runs home. "Call the fire department!" he yells to his wife. Then he hurries back to try and save Peggy. He grabs the back door handle and pulls. "Oh, no!" The door is locked!

The neighbor cups his hands around his

eyes and looks through a window. He can't see a thing in the smoke-filled house. He bangs on the glass with his fist. "Peggy! Come, Peggy!" he calls.

But Peggy doesn't come.

Minutes later, the Shaws arrive at Nana's house. Mr. Shaw's cell phone rings. He flips it open. "Hello."

"Tony! Your house . . . Your house is on fire!" his neighbor yells.

Our house is on fire? The news is so shocking that Mr. Shaw can't take it in. He starts to ask a question, but the neighbor interrupts.

"Peggy is in there," he says. "She's howling and screaming, and I can't get her out. The door is locked. Oh, Tony, it's dreadful to hear."

"Hold on. We're coming."

Mr. Shaw tells his wife and mother the awful news. The kids are out of the room and cannot hear. "Go," Nana says. "I'll watch the boys." Mr. and Mrs. Shaw jump into their car and speed toward home.

Meanwhile, heat and smoke are still building up inside their house. A red fire truck arrives on the scene with its siren screaming. Two firefighters leap to the ground and race toward the house. *Are people trapped inside?* A fireman smashes through the door with an ax. Then in they go, dragging a fire hose.

The firemen can see the stove in the light from the flames. *Sploosh!* They spray it with water. The flames die down. Now the smoke makes it dark as night. The firemen find their way by touch. They make a map of doorways and chairs in their heads so they can get back out.

First they climb the stairs and search the bedrooms. There's no one there. They go back through the living room and into the bathroom. Firefighter Martin Kammeier feels around for the toilet and sink. He puts his hand in the tub. Whoa! He feels something. It's soft and furry.

It's a dog!

What is a dog doing in the bathtub? Martin realizes she was trying to breathe through the drain. Poor Peggy. She doesn't know that the U-shaped pipe connection to the drain prevents gases—and fresh air— from entering the house.

Martin searches some more. Nothing.

He carries Peggy outside. She is limp as a noodle, and her tongue is hanging out. He drops her motionless body on the ground and runs back into the house. He has to finish putting out the fire.

Firefighter Stephen Buglass is outside setting up medical equipment in case it is needed. Stephen is a highly trained emergency worker. He once belonged to the best rescue team in all of England. The trouble is he usually works on humans. He does not expect to be handed a dog.

Stephen knows most fire victims do not die of burns. They die from breathing in smoke. Peggy spent over ten minutes inside the burning house. Her lungs must be full of deadly ash. The firefighter doubts he can save her. He thinks it's hopeless.

Trust the Nose

Dogs have super noses. Their sense of smell is 100,000 times better than a human's. To understand how good that is, imagine an Olympic-size swimming pool full of water. Then imagine stirring in a spoonful of sugar. A dog could smell the difference.

Specially trained dogs can sniff out bombs, drugs, harmful mold, and bedbugs. They can track down criminals and find missing kids.

Now dogs are learning to smell sickness. They can tell if people have cancer by smelling their breath. That's right. Your lovable pooch may be a doctor on four legs.

Peggy sits in the burnt bathtub where she was found during the fire.

Chapter 3

GOOD DOG

Firefighter Stephen Buglass looks at the oxygen mask in his equipment. The mask is designed for people and doesn't fit a dog's pointy face. He pulls off the mask and sticks its tube down the dog's throat. His partner turns on the oxygen and holds the tube in place.

Stephen places one hand over the other and pushes up and down on the dog's heart. This is hard work. Beads of sweat form on Stephen's forehead as he pushes almost 100 times a minute. A small crowd gathers to watch. Everyone wonders the same thing. Will the sweet-looking puppy come back to life?

Ten minutes pass. Twenty. Thirty. The fireman's arms feel heavy. He can't pump this dog's heart much longer. The animal hasn't moved. Stephen is ready to quit.

Then he notices something. It can't be. But it is! Inside Peggy's open mouth her gums are turning pink! That means her blood is moving again.

Stephen feels a new burst of energy. He ignores his shaky arms and keeps trying to restart Peggy's heart. When the oxygen runs out, his partner opens a second bottle.

More time passes. The crowd falls silent. Everyone is rooting for Peggy.

Finally, Stephen sees the puppy's chest rise. She is breathing on her own!

He stops pumping Peggy's heart and pulls the tube out of her throat. He holds the tube so that oxygen blows over the dog's face. Then he watches . . . and waits.

Mr. and Mrs. Shaw arrive home to see thick, black smoke billowing out of their house.

"It's unreal!" Mr. Shaw says. Two fire trucks and a police car are parked out front. Firefighters wearing bright yellow helmets and yellow-striped, gold uniforms swarm over their lawn. They are rolling up flat fire hoses. Groups of neighbors are walking around staring and talking.

A fireman shows Mr. Shaw the busted door and takes him through the house. Mrs. Shaw barely notices the damage. She runs from person to person asking, "Our dog? What about our dog?"

Much later Curtis learns what happened. By then his tired father is asleep on Nana's couch. His mother is driving him and Daniel to a neighbor's house to sleep. "Why are we going there?" Curtis asks. "Why don't we just go home?"

As gently as she can, Mrs. Shaw explains that Peggy accidentally started a fire. She tells them their house has been badly damaged and needs to be repaired.

She tells them Peggy is alive but at the vet.

Curtis shakes his head. "I don't believe you, Mommy." Deep inside he fears he can never go home again. And he is scared for Peggy. Maybe she has already died and his mom hasn't told him. Or, almost as bad, maybe everybody is mad at her.

Peggy did a bad thing. She started a fire that ruined his family's couch, TV, and video game player. Curtis worries. *If naughty Peggy is okay, will Daddy send her away? If he does, what will I do without her?*

Two days after the fire, Mrs. Shaw takes Curtis to visit their home. Together they wander about inside. Since black dust covers the windows, they use a flashlight to see. Curtis gasps at the ruined walls and melted refrigerator door. He looks up at the hole the firemen chopped in the kitchen ceiling and down at the chunks of ceiling lying at his feet. Everything stinks of smoke and burnt plastic. Curtis chokes on the smell and holds his nose. But even with his nose plugged, a bad taste fills his mouth.

For six long weeks, Mrs. Shaw and the boys live at friends' houses. Mr. Shaw stays at Nana's. He drives a truck during the day and works on the house until late every night. When Peggy leaves the vet, she stays with him. The vet warns Mr. Shaw to wake up often and poke the dog during the night to make sure she keeps breathing. Mr. Shaw does exactly that—no matter how tired he feels.

The next morning Mr. Shaw finds a

big, black stain on Nana's white carpet. The stain is right beside Peggy's open mouth. It comes from her breathing out the smoke that still clogs her lungs.

Ever so slowly things begin to get better. Mr. Shaw finishes his work on the house and buys a new television. It is not as big as the one that burned, but it works fine. The family finally moves back home, and Peggy begins to act like herself again. The family is happy. It hasn't been the same without her silly stunts.

One day Curtis takes Peggy outside to play in the yard. He throws a soccer ball for her to chase. To his delight she runs after it like she used to before the fire. Peggy grabs the ball with her mouth.

Then *POP!* Her sharp teeth poke a hole

in the ball and it goes flat.

Curtis freezes. He looks back at his
watching parents. Will they be mad at
Peggy for ruining his ball?

No. Mr. and Mrs. Shaw are smiling
and laughing. "Don't worry," says Curtis's
dad. "We will buy you another one."

Curtis smiles and hugs his best friend.
The truth is, Peggy always means to be
good. She just forgets sometimes. So
whether she's been naughty or nice,
one thing will never change. Everybody
loves Peggy.

Get Out and Stay Out!

Never go back inside a burning building. These words of advice come from Sparky the spotted Dalmatian. Sparky is the official mascot of the National Fire Protection Association and for good reason. Dalmatians have lived in firehouses since horses pulled fire wagons. These canine long-distance runners raced alongside the team leading the way. Just as important, they kept the horses calm.

So listen to Sparky. He gives doggone good advice.

Super sneaky and stealthy, Olivia sets off on one of her nightly raids.

OLIVIA: THE CAT BURGLAR

Olivia might look like a sweet little kitty, but this sneaky cat leads a secret life of crime.

Spring 2009, Milford, Connecticut

livia. Charged with more than 400 counts of robbery and holding on to stolen goods.

Also known as: Cow Kitty

Description: White with black spots, all-black ears, and black tail.

Scars and Marks: Beard-like black smudge under her chin.

Habits: A sneaky thief who goes to work when no one is looking, especially under cover of darkness.

Likes stuffed sharks and usually steals gloves in pairs.

Status: Last seen hiding out in Anne and Richard Weizel's backyard, in Milford, Connecticut. Warning! Suspect is unarmed and adorable.

Olivia, the little 8-pound (3.6 kg) kitty, leads a double life. During the day she plays the role of devoted house pet to the Weizels' sons—Josh, ten, and Jeremy, eight. But when the sun goes down, *beware!* This fluffy kitty turns into a sticky-footed thief. With one goal in mind, she scrambles over wooden fences and cuts through backyards. She prowls through the woods and prances across darkened streets. Every night she drags her loot home.

This feline crime spree begins when Anne Weizel convinces her husband, a newspaper reporter, that they should adopt a cat. To find one, Mrs. Weizel visits the "cat lady."

The cat lady takes in strays and finds them homes. Nearly twenty black, yellow, and tabby cats laze about her living room. They lie curled on the couch and stretched out on the floor. Fat cats and skinny cats. Old cats and baby cats.

The kitties rub against Mrs. Weizel's legs and make soft, rumbly, purring sounds. She pets first one, then another. It is so hard to choose. Finally, she scoops up a boy kitty and presses him against her cheek. "I want this one," she says.

Mrs. Weizel puts the kitten into a

plastic cat carrier as another scampers past. "That's his sister," the cat lady says.

Mrs. Weizel blinks. *Really?* The girl kitten immediately appeals to her. She loves its black and white coloring and dainty size. The little furry ball could fit inside a teacup. And the kitten's eyes! They're almond-shaped. Anne can't help herself. She takes both kittens.

At home, Josh and Jeremy squeal happily at the news of getting two kitties.

But Mr. Weizel looks into the cat carrier and sees four glowing eyes staring back. He groans. "You were supposed to get just one."

"Yes, but . . ." Mrs. Weizel tries to explain. She opens the carrier, and both kitties run for cover. The boy cat hides behind the couch. The girl cat scoots down to the cellar and disappears in a pile of boxes.

"We agreed on *one* cat only," Mr. Weizel says, throwing his hands in the air. "Please take the second one back."

Mrs. Weizel sighs. She wants both cats, but a deal is a deal. She will return the girl kitty as soon as she can catch her. Mrs. Weizel sets out some food. Overnight the food disappears, but the scared kitten remains out of sight.

Josh tries to get her to come out by dangling a string. Jeremy dishes up more food. "Here kitty, kitty . . ." Mrs. Weizel calls. Nothing works.

Two weeks pass.

The boy cat is getting used to his home. Mrs. Weizel puts him in the cellar hoping he can get his sister to come out. He does. When Mr. Weizel sees the girl kitten up close, he gives up. "She *is* kind of cute," he says. "I guess she can stay."

Mrs. Weizel names the boy Gabby and the girl Olivia. "Olivia fits," Mrs. Weizel says, "because she is so dainty and sweet. She looks like she should be taking piano lessons and attending school in France."

Once Olivia decides to join the family, she joins it in a big way. The little kitty with the big heart does not play favorites. She snuggles with everyone. She seems especially determined to win over Mr. Weizel. The dog-loving man of the house usually tries to avoid cats, but Olivia refuses to be ignored. She hops into Mr. Weizel's lap when he reads the newspaper. She winds around his legs when he stands in the kitchen. She curls up on his feet when he lies down.

Before long, Olivia rules all the animals in the house. That includes her big brother and two shy, droopy-eared beagles. Every day, Mrs. Weizel takes the dogs for a mile-long walk. Olivia not only insists on joining them. She leads the way, except when she sees a dog she doesn't know. Then Olivia darts behind a bush until the dog passes.

One freezing winter morning, knee-high snow is piled along the sidewalk. Mrs. Weizel and the dogs barely get started out the door before Olivia spots them leaving. Immediately the cat scoots in front of them. Holding her tail up high, she walks along like she is the boss of the world.

Every time the dogs stop to sniff or pee, Olivia stands and waits. When the beagles start walking, so does she. One dog dares to try moving ahead. *Yelp!* Olivia swats him. The beagle tucks his tail between his legs and slinks to the end of the line.

Neighbors notice Olivia leading the way. All along the street, they leave their breakfasts and hurry to their windows to watch the show. No one guesses that the leader of this strange parade has a secret —she is a cat burglar.

The Secret Life of Cats

What do cats do all day when they're home alone? Sleep? That's what most people think. But scientist Jill Villarreal wanted the real scoop. She gave "cat cams" to fifty house cats. The cat cams hung from their collars and snapped a photo every 15 minutes. Jill then studied the best 777 pictures. Guess what? When the family's away, the cat will play. Or watch TV. Or hang out with the dog. To Jill's surprise, kitties home alone take very few cat naps. Mostly they peer out windows! Maybe they're watching for you to come home.

Olivia sniffs a large pile of her "loot."

Mrs. Weizel returns home from work one day and hears meowing coming from under her bed. She kneels down to look and finds Olivia and four tiny kittens. When the kittens are old enough, Mrs. Weizel gives three of them away. She keeps one. He grows bigger than his mother, but Olivia is still the boss.

Still nobody suspects her of doing anything wrong. Not even when Mrs. Weizel finds a gardening glove dropped on her front porch.

Hmm, she thinks. *A neighbor must have found it and thought it belonged to us.* The next day, another glove appears. Then another, and another. Every day for three months, Mrs. Weizel discovers a new glove lying on the steps. Every day she picks it up and tosses it in the washing machine with the rest of the laundry. She puts all the gloves in a large plastic garbage bag. *But who is leaving them?* Little did she know, the answer was right under her feet.

One day Jeremy and a friend are outside playing when Olivia appears carrying something in her mouth.

She drops the package in the grass, and Jeremy rushes over and picks it up. It is surprisingly heavy.

Jeremy runs inside and shows his mom. "Look what Olivia dragged home!" He unrolls a strip of cloth pockets holding a mini wrench, screwdrivers, and other tools.

Mrs. Weizel barely looks at the mini tool kit. She has other things on her mind.

Not wanting to be bothered with silly cat stories, Mrs. Weizel shoos Jeremy away. She is thinking about her mother, who has been very sick.

Later that evening, Mrs. Weizel happens to look out the window and spots Olivia crossing the street. The cat waddles slightly as she walks and keeps her front legs wide apart. Mrs. Weizel squints and leans forward. "Well, I'll be!" A stolen garden glove dangles from Olivia's mouth!

So Olivia is bringing the gloves home. But why?

Mrs. Weizel stops worrying to think. How far does Olivia roam to find all these gloves? Does she mistake gloves for birds, squirrels, or some other animal? Does she think they are cat toys? Or is she stealing because she misses her kittens? Maybe Olivia simply enjoys collecting gloves, like some humans collect stamps or rare coins. Mrs. Weizel adds this glove to the dozens of others in her garbage bag. What a strange habit. Mrs. Weizel continues to think it over.

Did You Know?

A group of cats is called a clowder.

One evening Olivia sits beside her food dish washing her face. Mrs. Weizel comes into the kitchen. She does not pet or even notice the cat. She just flops down at the kitchen table across from her husband. In her mother's house, a vase of freshly cut roses would be sitting on the table, but not here. Mrs. Weizel's table is covered with bills. Her husband will pay the most important ones. Others will have to wait.

Mr. Weizel looks up from the piles of paper. "What's wrong?" he asks.

"It's my mother," Mrs. Weizel says. "The doctor is starting her on treatments." After a pause, she adds, "Another bill collector called today."

Josh hears his parents talking and fears an argument is beginning. His parents fight a lot lately, and it scares Josh to hear them. Their angry words make his stomach hurt. Today he escapes by running upstairs to his room and lying down on his bed. Olivia must sense that he is upset. She goes upstairs with him and snuggles beside him. Josh pets her. The warm feel of her furry little body against his fingers makes him feel better.

Right now Olivia acts like she doesn't have a care in the world. She licks her paw and rubs it over her face. Then she stretches and purrs. But the kitty must be thinking something, because that night she suddenly changes her routine. Forget the gardening gloves, Olivia is sick of those. She is after bigger loot.

Why do cats steal?

Scientists disagree. Some believe that "cat burglars" are not so much stealing as they are collecting. They think some kitties like certain things and can't help but add them to their stash. For these cats, it may be all about the hunt.

Other scientists think bringing home socks and toys is simply normal cat behavior. Stray cats drag home food to feed their kittens. Tame ones often bring their owners dead birds or mice. Cat burglars just get carried away—maybe because they like the attention.

She brings home a Winnie-the-Pooh purse, some rubber bands, and a yellow sponge.

A few days later, the loot gets even bigger. A stuffed shark with googly eyes, a matching pair of socks, sunglasses, and an oven mitt. Olivia begins showing great pride in her collection. She no longer drops them on the front porch and leaves. Instead, she sits beside them and meows—loudly, until someone comes to see what she's brought. "She doesn't stop until I open the door, pick her up, and kiss her," Mrs. Weizel says. Even if it is one o'clock in the morning, which it often is."

As the seasons change, the loot gets larger and larger. That spring Olivia finds a dust mop. Summer brings swim goggles and a beach ball. Running shoes turn up in the fall. Earmuffs, mittens, and a hand-knit Christmas tree ornament arrive in winter.

Meanwhile the family grows shorter of money. The bills keep piling up, and there's no money to pay them.

One day Mrs. Weizel steps outside to find a lady's big, black bra stretched across her front walk. She bursts into laughter. Then she carries the bra inside and waves it in front of Olivia's face. "You naughty kitty. Did you steal this?"

But Olivia is one cool cat. She shows no guilt. She just lies on her side blinking her almond-shaped eyes and twitching her soft, fluffy tail. Mrs. Weizel pets Olivia's long outstretched back. She could never resist that cuddly kitty.

The Weizels set up a "lost and found" box so neighbors can come get their stolen belongings.

"STOLEN" TREASURE

Mrs. Weizel makes her friends laugh with stories of Olivia's thefts. Even better, it cheers up her mother. One Sunday Mrs. Weizel even stands up in church and admits that her sweet-looking pussycat is really a furry thief.

Word gets around about the four-legged burglar living on Ard Court. Neighbors who are missing things come by and paw through a "lost and found" box of Olivia's loot. One man makes repeated trips to take back a pair of expensive leather work gloves. He leaves them outside on the patio table because they get so dirty. He tries to ruin Olivia's plan by piling tools on top of them. But two can play at that game. The crooked feline his kids call "Cow Kitty" simply tugs the gloves out from underneath.

Meanwhile, the family's troubles go from bad to worse. Mr. Weizel loses his newspaper job and Mrs. Weizel's mother passes away. Every family member feels sad and upset.

Mrs. Weizel worries more than ever. She earns some money as a substitute teacher, but it is not enough. With her husband out of work, how will they pay for doctor appointments? For food? For clothing?

Mr. Weizel looks for a new job. At home he reads help-wanted ads on the Internet. Then he goes to the library to find more ads in the newspapers. Every day he calls reporters that he knows, people he used to work with. "Have you heard of any jobs?" he asks. They always answer, "No."

One day Mr. Weizel checks on a job near where he used to work. No luck. His shoulders slump as he climbs back into his car to drive home. He only drives a few blocks before his car sputters to a stop. Mr. Weizel looks at the dashboard of his car. Its gas pump symbol glows yellow.

"Oh, no!" Mr. Weizel grits his teeth and bangs his fist on the steering wheel.

So much is going wrong. First he gets behind on his bills. Then he loses his job. Now he runs out of gas. He doesn't know how this day could get any worse, or any better for that matter.

Mr. Weizel looks sad when he finally walks into the house. But he can't stay that way—not when his wife shows him two soggy rolls of toilet paper that Olivia had dragged home in the rain. "She delivered these at 2 a.m. And she looked so proud," says Mrs. Weizel. Mr. Weizel took the soggy rolls in his hand. Husband and wife cried with

Did You Know?

Cats have great night vision. In the dark they can see about six times better than humans.

laughter. It was the first time they felt happy in a while.

Like a faithful mail carrier, neither rain nor snow keeps Olivia from her rounds. Mr. Weizel admired her for always going out and getting the job done . . . even though she was stealing.

"You never give up, do you?" he asks the cat. "You just keep on trucking, going out every day and finding us stuff."

Mr. Weizel perks up. He makes a decision right then. He would work as hard at finding a job as Olivia does searching for presents. Every morning he wakes up curious to see what Olivia has brought.

His new attitude helps. Several months later he receives an email from an online newspaper. Would he like to work for them?

"I sure would!" Mr. Weizel writes back. The next day he packs up his camera and computer. On the way out the door he steps over a child's green flip-flop that Olivia had left on the step. Then off he goes with a smile on his face.

The whole family cheers up to see Dad back at work. Even Olivia seems happy. Her stealing continues for a while, but she no longer drags home two or three items a night. Some nights she doesn't bring anything home. Olivia stops bringing home gardening gloves completely until one night . . .

Mrs. Weizel is having a terrible day. Her car won't start, and she gets to work late. Once she arrives the kids she is teaching won't do their work. When she gets home, her own kids argue and complain. Most of all, Mrs. Weizel misses her mother. She wishes she had some of her mother's sweet-smelling rose bushes growing in her own yard. Just looking at them would boost her spirits.

Olivia climbs into her lap. Mrs. Weizel strokes her silky, soft fur and tries not to cry.

That night Olivia goes back on the job. A year had passed since she last brought home a gardening glove. And it had been several days since she brought home anything. But now the cuddly kitty sets off on one more hunt.

The sun is up before Mrs. Weizel hears Olivia's familiar meow. It's the tone that says, "Come look what I found for you."

Mrs. Weizel opens the front door and finds Olivia bearing a muddy glove.

"Thank you, Olivia," Mrs. Weizel says. She grasps one finger of the filthy glove and carries it to the washing machine. She throws it in. It swishes around with the rest of the load. Later, Mrs. Weizel removes the spanking clean glove and gasps in surprise.

It is off-white, cotton, and decorated with . . . red roses! Her mother's favorite!

Mrs. Weizel picks up Olivia and hugs her. She pins the glove to her bulletin board. "It comforts me to look at it," she says.

Olivia hardly ever hunts anymore. But what if she returns to a life of crime? What should the Weizels do then?

Doctor Cat

Feeling sad or afraid? Get a cat. You don't even have to pet it. Research shows that just having one around will calm you.

Dennis Turner is an animal behaviorist at Switzerland's University of Zurich. He says, "The fantastic thing about the cat is that it doesn't force itself on the person." A cat is there when you need it, but understands when you want to be alone.

Cats comfort depressed people. They help them make friends. And they lower their blood pressure. What could be more purr-fect?

They could sentence her to community service. A cat burglar in California rode in a parade to help the humane society raise money.

They could keep Olivia in the house if they wanted to put an end to her career once and for all.

But rather than get mad at their kitty for her strange behavior, the Weizels love her for it. Even when she brings home toilet paper. To them, it's not the gift. It's the thought that counts.

THE END

DON'T MISS!

NATIONAL GEOGRAPHIC
KIDS **CHAPTERS**

DOG FINDS LOST DOLPHINS!

And More True
Stories of
Amazing
Animal
Heroes

By Elizabeth Carney

NATIONAL GEOGRAPHIC

**Turn the page
for a sneak preview . . .**

Scientists do not always know why dolphins and whales get stranded.

CALL FOR HELP

When Chris Blankenship got an emergency call to report to the beach, he expected it to be busy. And it was!

About 80 dolphins were wriggling and squeaking in the shallow water. A small army of people worked quickly to help them. Team leaders barked orders. Volunteers put on wet suits for their turn in the water. News reporters were there too. They were looking for a big story.

Chris is a dolphin expert. He has seen dolphins and whales stuck on shore before. This time was different. Usually one or two dolphins get stuck in shallow water. Sometimes they get stuck in the twisty roots of mangrove trees. *But 80 dolphins!* Chris thought. *With so many, how do we know that we've found them all?*

Every time a dolphin or whale gets stranded, it is a race against time. The sooner the dolphins are found, the easier it can be to save them. Chris ran his hands over a dolphin's smooth, rubbery skin. He thought how odd it was that such a good swimmer needed help.

Dolphins are perfect for the underwater world. With their strong bodies and sleek fins, they can swim seven times faster than humans. They can hold their breath for more than 15 minutes and dive 2,000 feet (610 m) underwater.

Dolphins are also very smart. They hunt in groups. They make up games to play. They even name themselves using whistling sounds. Many researchers spend their lives learning how dolphins communicate. In a dolphin's world, every click, whistle, and gesture has a meaning.

Yet sometimes dolphins end up in trouble. They can get stuck on a beach. It's a dangerous situation for them. By the time they are found, most stranded dolphins are sick or have died already.

Why would such smart animals swim so close to a beach? We don't really know. Maybe some stranded dolphins were sick. Maybe pollution in the water confused them. Maybe they got lost during a storm at sea.

In order to find the answer, scientists study stranded dolphins as they try to help them. They look for clues that will help them keep dolphins safe.

Chris and the animal doctors got to work on the stranded dolphins. The first step: Make sure the dolphin can breathe. Dolphins are mammals, like humans. They have lungs and need to breathe air. They take in air through a blowhole on their back, behind their head.

The stranded dolphins were very tired. They couldn't stay up on their bellies or swim on their own. People took turns holding the animals up so they could breathe. They rested the dolphins on their knees to keep their blowholes above water.

The volunteers also kept the dolphins' skin moist by splashing water on their bodies. A dolphin's exposed skin can dry out quickly in the hot Florida sun.

A team examined each dolphin. They had to find out which dolphins were healthy enough to survive in the wild. The healthiest dolphins were helped back to deeper water right away. Sick dolphins were taken to a special hospital. There they were given medicine and food.

Chris popped a fish stuffed with medicine in a dolphin's mouth.

This one is in rough shape, but it seems like a fighter, he thought. Suddenly, a shout got Chris's attention.

"Chris!" yelled a volunteer. "Quick! Come over here!"

Chris ran down the beach to a spot full of mangrove trees. A small group of dolphins were stuck in the trees' thick roots. They must have been separated from the main group. Now it was too late. They were too sick to save.

Chris sighed. *I wish we had some way of locating dolphins. Then we could get to them sooner.*

After that day, Chris kept thinking about what he had seen. He wondered if there was a better way to find lost dolphins. Then Chris started reading about some dogs that worked nearby. They were trained to search for people who get lost on or near the water. The dogs worked along beaches or from boats in the water. They sniffed the air for the missing person's smell. They could even smell objects that were slightly underwater.

Chris wondered: *If dogs can find humans in the water, can they find dolphins too?*

WANT TO KNOW WHAT HAPPENS NEXT?
Be sure to check out *Dog Finds Lost Dolphins!*
Available wherever books and ebooks are sold.

INDEX

MORE INFORMATION

To find more information about the animal species featured in this book, check out these books and websites:

Face to Face With Orangutans,
National Geographic, 2011

Cats vs. Dogs,
National Geographic, 2009

National Geographic Kids "Creature Features: Orangutans"
kids.nationalgeographic.com/kids/animals/creaturefeature/
orangutan

Orangutan Foundation International
www.orangutan.org

National Geographic "Animals: Domestic Cat"
animals.nationalgeographic.com/animals/mammals/domestic-cat

National Geographic Kids "Games: Brainteasers Cool Cats"
kids.nationalgeographic.com/kids/games/puzzlesquizzes/
brainteasercoolcat

National Geographic Kids "Photos: Dogs With Jobs"
kids.nationalgeographic.com/
kids/photos/dogs-with-jobs

National Geographic "Animals: Domestic Dog"
animals.nationalgeographic
.com/animals/mammals/
domestic-dog

This book is dedicated to my own partner in crime, my husband, Neil.
—Aline Alexander Newman

CREDITS

Cover, Cyril Ruoso; 4-5, Dr. Lee G. Simmons, Omaha's Henry Doorly Zoo; 6, Life on White/Alamy; 6 (background), Elenathewise/Dreamstime; 13, Lisa Turay/iStockphoto.com; 16, Omaha World-Herald; 25, David Allen Brandt/Getty Images; 25, Sonica83/Dreamstime; 26, Frans Lanting/National Geographic Stock; 34, Konrad Wothe/SuperStock; 36, Lorraine Shaw; 38, Lorraine Shaw; 47, Cynoclub/Dreamstime; 48, North News & Pictures Ltd.; 57, Gvictoria/Dreamstime; 58, North News & Pictures Ltd.; 67, Minden/SuperStock; 68, Autumn Driscoll; 70, Autumn Driscoll; 79, 0007filip/Dreamstime; 80, Autumn Driscoll; 89, Tzooka/Dreamstime; 90, Autumn Driscoll; 99, Atm2003/Dreamstime; 101, Bill Sumner; 102, Tony Ashby/AFP/Getty Images; 111, Life on White/Alamy; 111 (background), Elenathewise/Dreamstime

ACKNOWLEDGMENTS

A special thanks to:

Tracey Marshall and Stephen Buglass, for their invaluable detective work.

Amy and Steve Stevens, for adding to cat burglar lore.

Hope Irvin Marston, Jean Capron, Judy Ann Grant, Jeanne Converse, and Jule Lattimer, for critiquing my first draft.

Lee G. Simmons, DVM, for unearthing his photos of Fu Manchu.

Geza Teleki, for wise advice and moral support.

Regina Brooks, for handling the business end.

The National Geographic staff, especially Catherine Hughes, for recommending me to the Book Division, and Becky Baines, for never giving up on Fu Manchu.

I am grateful to the following experts:

Bonnie Beaver, DVM, Texas A&M University College of Veterinary Medicine

PD Dr. sc. Dennis C. Turner, Owner and Director of I.E.T./I.E.A.P., Hirzel, Switzerland

Suzanne Hetts, Ph.D., Animal Behavior Associates, Inc., Littleton, CO

Lori Perkins, Chairperson of AZA Orangutan Species Survival Plan and Director of Animal Programs at Zoo Atlanta

Above all, I thank the animal-loving families, brave firemen, and devoted zoo personnel for graciously sharing their stories with me. They made this project possible.